ALPHONSE MARIA MUCHA

ILSÉE

48 Full-Color Plates From Mucha's Art Nouveau Masterpiece

Dover Publications, Inc.

NEW YORK

PUBLISHER'S NOTE

By common consent, the greatest illustrated book by the Czech-born Art Nouveau master Alphonse Maria Mucha (1860–1939) is his 1897 *Ilsée, Princesse de Tripoli*. The commission for it resulted from his poster work in Paris for Sarah Bernhardt, which had begun in late 1894. One of his 1895 posters for the actress featured her in the title role of Edmond Rostand's play *La Princesse lointaine*, based on the twelfth-century troubadour Jaufré Rudel's legendary love for a distant princess he had never met. The art publisher H. Piazza wanted Mucha to illustrate an edition of the play, but Rostand requested too high a fee, and the task of writing a substitute text on the same subject was given to the young Robert de Flers (1872–1927), later an adroit author of stage comedies.

In de Flers's brief novel, Jaufré is a chaste youth, devoted to nature and the Virgin, but obsessed with the phantom of a magnificent young woman. When local pilgrims, returning to Jaufré's castle from the Holy Land, report on their visit to Tripoli in North Africa and describe the princess who sheltered them there, Jaufré recognizes in their words the woman of his visions and sets sail for her land. Ilsée, on her part, had also had premonitions of Jaufré's existence. Jaufré dies in Tripoli right after the two meet, and Ilsée enters a convent.

Mucha was a heaven-sent artist for this type of material, which perfectly suited all his artistic tastes and strengths: his love for medieval and Byzantine trappings; his adoration of nature; his troubling blend of religiosity and carnality (his best-drawn female figures are usually hieratic harlots or sensual saints); and, above all, his matchless feeling for design. The more than 130 lithographs he created for *Ilsée* are incredibly inventive, with no border exactly repeated, and with a wealth of floral, animal, geometric and other ornament lavished everywhere.

The present selection of 48 plates (in addition to the original title-page border), reproduced directly from a copy of the extremely rare first edition, concentrates on the more highly designed and ornamented pages (borders, bands, frames) rather than the more purely illustrative ones. The original French text has been dropped out, leaving blank areas easily adaptable to advertising and other commercial uses. This monument of Art Nouveau color ornament is thus made widely available for the first time.

Published in Canada by General Publishing Company, Ltd., 30 Lesmill Road, Don Mills, Toronto, Ontario.
Published in the United Kingdom by Constable and Company, Ltd., 10 Orange Street, London WC2H 7EG.

This Dover edition, first published in 1983, contains 48 illustrated pages (plus the original title border) from the novel *Ilsée, Princesse de Tripoli*, by Robert de Flers, originally published in an edition of 252 copies by L'Edition d'Art/H. Piazza & Cie, Paris, 1897. The Publisher's Note was written specially for the present edition.

Manufactured in the United States of America
Dover Publications, Inc., 31 East 2nd Street, Mineola, N.Y. 11501

Library of Congress Cataloging in Publication Data

Mucha, Alphonse Marie, 1860-1939.
Ilsée : 48 full-color plates from Mucha's art nouveau masterpiece.

"Illustrated pages from the novel Ilsée, princesse de Tripoli by Robert de Flers, originally published . . . Paris, 1897"—Verso t.p.
1. Mucha, Alphonse Marie, 1860-1939. 2. Flers, Robert de, 1872-1927. Ilsée, princesse de Tripoli—Illustrations. 3. Decoration and ornament—Art nouveau. I. Flers, Robert de, 1872-1927. Ilsée, princesse de Tripoli. II. Title.
NC989.C92M822 1983 741.64'092'4 83-5320
ISBN 0-486-24542-X

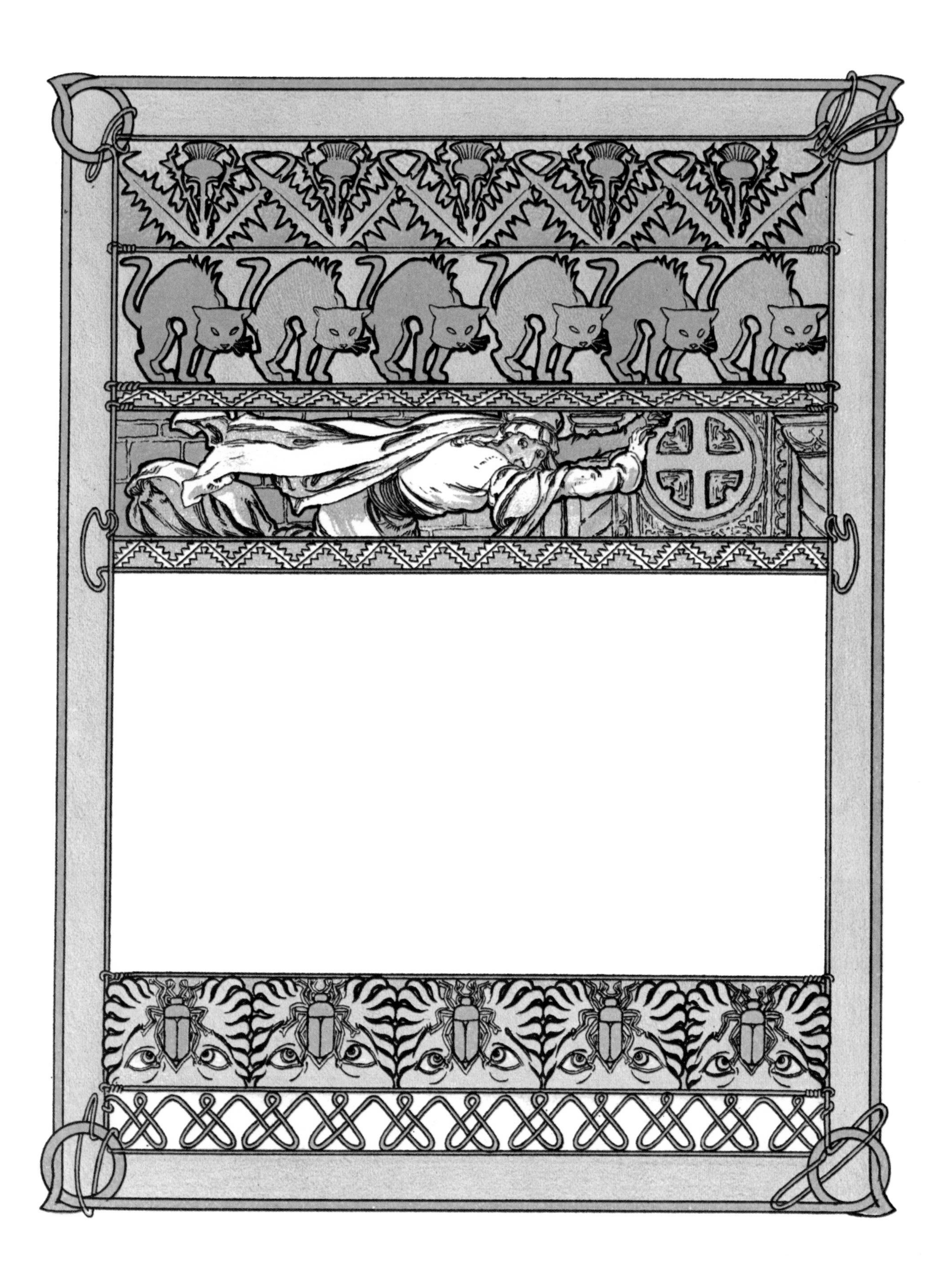

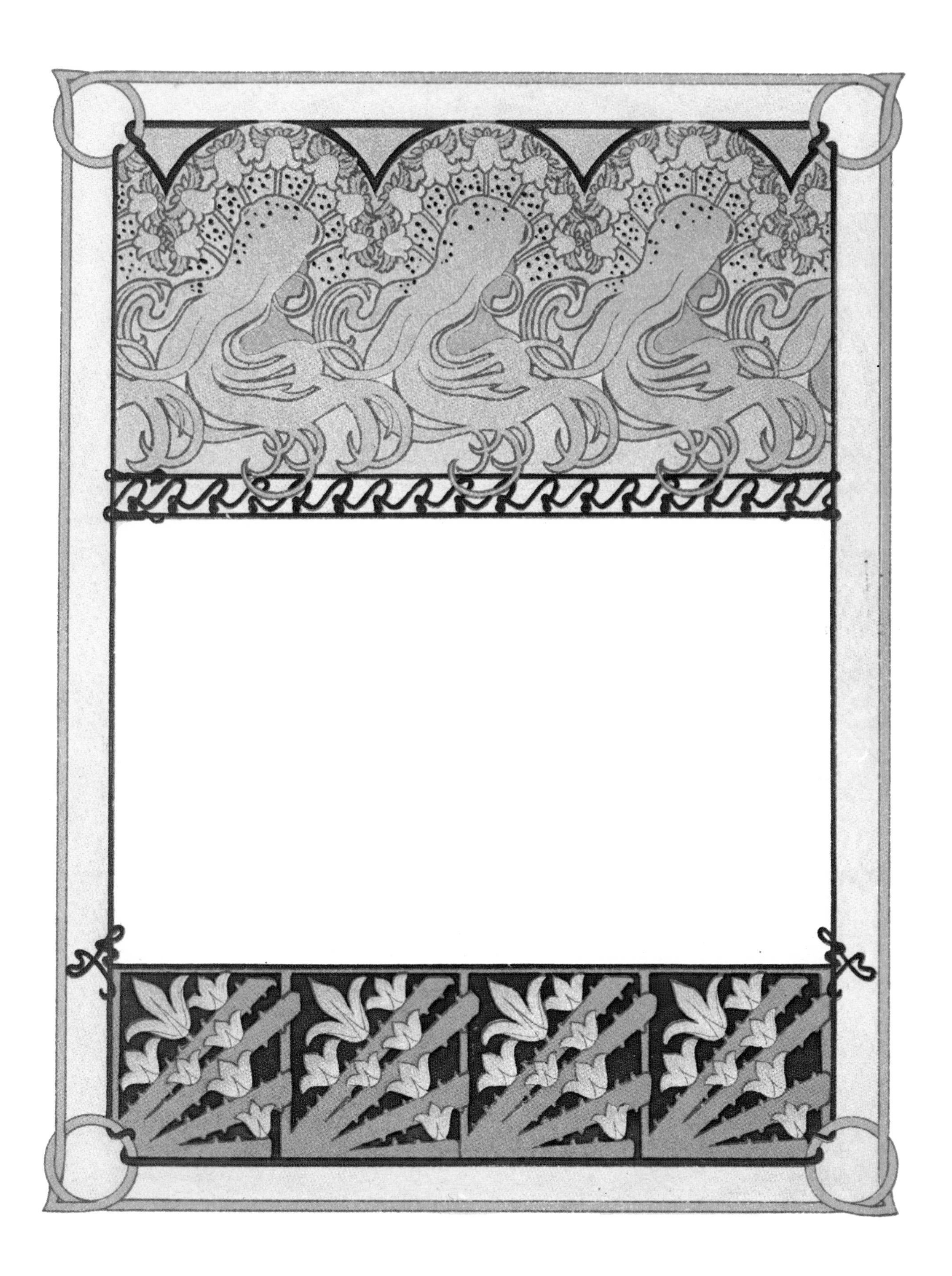

Mucha

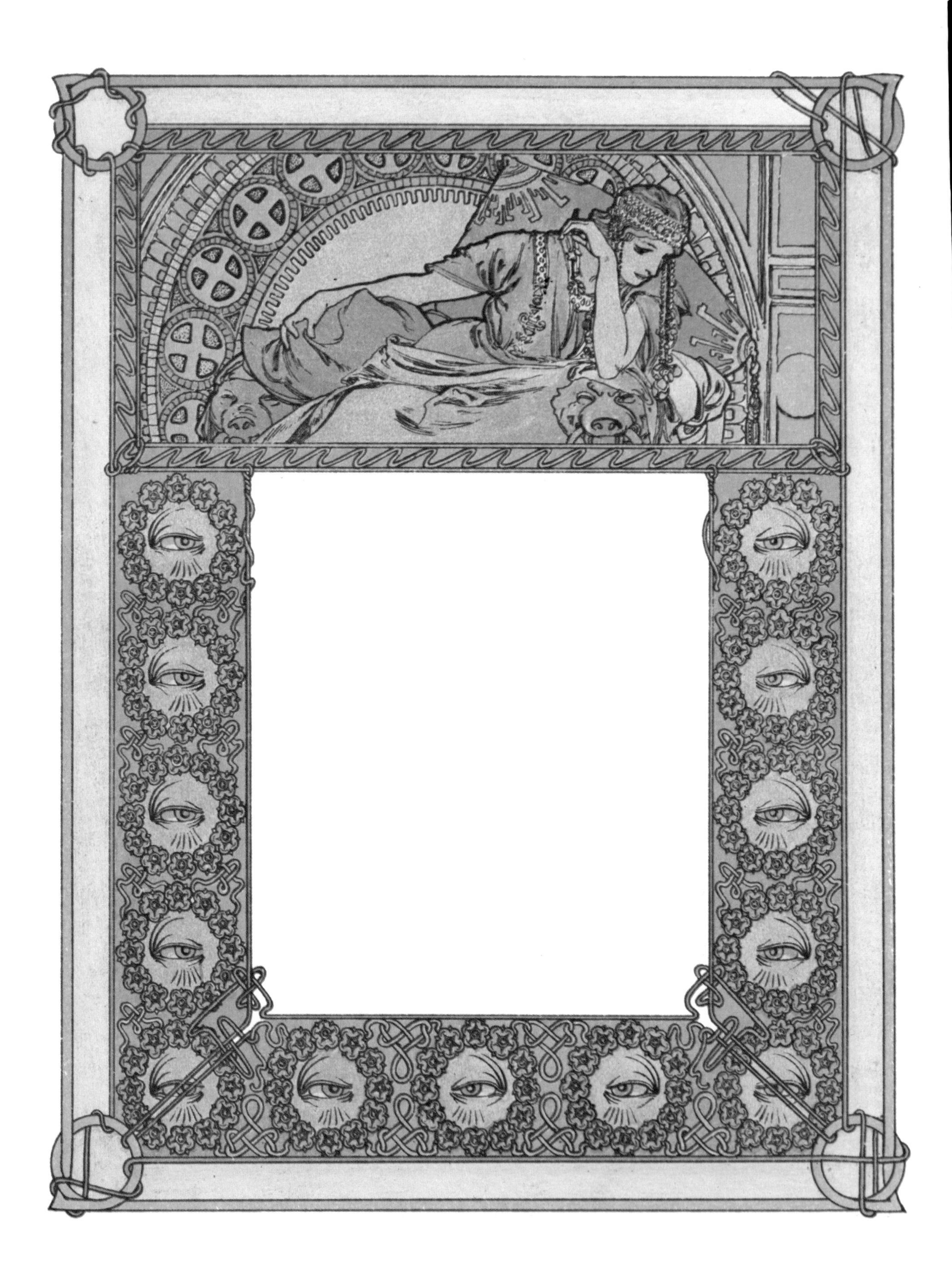